First published in 2008
© Demos. Some rights reserved
Magdalen House, 136 Tooley Street,
London, SE1 2TU, UK

ISBN 978 1 84180 199 5
Copy edited by Julie Pickard, London
Series design by modernactivity
Typeset by Chat Noir Design, Charente
Printed by Lecturis, Eindhoven

Set in Gotham Rounded
and Baskerville 10
Cover paper: Arctic Volume
Text paper: Munken Premium White

state of trust

Simon Parker
Phil Spires
Faizal Farook
Melissa Mean

DEMOS

Contents

Acknowledgements

We are grateful to Communities and Local Government and the Improvement and Development Agency for supporting this project. In particular, we would like to thank Ben Crowe, Richard Grice and Mark Rickard for providing support and advice throughout the research process.

This project would not have been possible without the enthusiastic participation of politicians and officers at our four partner councils. Special thanks are due to Sarah Buckler, Julie Collison, Lee Cranston, Richard Honeysett, Edward Knowles, Kevin Sheehan and Steve Stewart.

Many people have contributed valuable comments and ideas to this interim report. Perri 6 offered us advice beyond the call of duty, as did Alessandra Buonfino at Demos. Eddie Gibb, Noel Hatch and James Huckle provided invaluable support to the project in its early stages. Paul Skidmore played an important role in conceiving this piece of work.

The views expressed in this report are those of the authors and do not necessarily reflect those of either CLG or the IDeA. Any errors or omissions are our own.

Simon Parker
Phil Spires
Faizal Farook
Melissa Mean
July 2008

About this pamphlet

This interim report sets out the findings from the first phase of a major research project examining how local government can build more trusting relationships with its citizens.

The project has involved 20 focus groups with members of the public, eight workshops with council staff and a number of interviews with senior political and managerial figures. The work was carried out in four council areas: Lewisham, Solihull, Sunderland and Wakefield.

The main body of this report sets out an overview of the research to date, including information gathered from an extensive literature review. Our analysis and conclusions remain provisional and will be refined in a further phase of action research to test their application in practice.

1 Introduction

Trust – and its absence – preoccupies and concerns us. Trust knits society together and makes it possible for people to get on with their everyday lives. Without it, society would become impossible.
   Will Hutton[1]

*The government today are lying *********. At least in Thatcher's day you knew if she said something it would happen, you might not have liked it but at least you could trust her to do it.*
   Male, retired, C2D, Wakefield

Trust is one of the most important assets that a governing institution can possess. Its presence helps to foster democratic participation, economic success[2] and public sector efficiency. Its absence can lead to grinding battles between the state and its citizens, and sometimes to an outright refusal to participate in government activities.

In this study, we have tried to understand trust in local government – what it is, why it matters and how councils can develop more of it. Taking the working definition of trust as 'firm belief in the reliability, truth, ability or strength of someone or something'[3] we have carried out an extensive literature review as well as interviews and 20 focus groups with a nationally representative sample of the public in four local authority areas – Lewisham, Solihull, Sunderland and Wakefield.

Our conclusion is that the past decade's focus on service improvement has not been enough to gain more trust for local government. Councils also need to use the personal interactions between their staff and the public to build ongoing, two-way relationships with the people they serve based on honesty and reciprocity. At the same time, local politicians need to counter allegations of unfairness in their decision making by developing more robust and open processes for allocating resources.

This report is timely because of the current widespread concern about low levels of trust in government. The truth is that the UK does suffer from unusually low levels of trust – Britain ranks 22nd of the EU25 in terms of trust in government.[4] The number of people in England who said they trusted government fell five points to 18 per cent between 1994 and 2003.[5]

However, it is not clear that these figures represent a crisis of confidence – some polls indicate that our levels of trust in politicians have remained steady over the past 20 years.[6] Trust in some public sector professionals such as doctors and teachers has remained remarkably steady, with doctors currently at their highest levels of trust since the early 1980s.[7]

A similar picture emerges in local government – we know that trust is low, but there is no evidence that it is in critical decline. Only 43 per cent of the public trust councillors to tell the truth and just 36 per cent trust senior council managers, but these levels have remained steady over the past few years. Local politicians are still more trusted than government ministers, business leaders and broadsheet journalists.[8] Our research suggests that people remain attached to the ideal of public service, and indeed to the principle of local self-governance, but are often frustrated with the reality.

Rather than a straightforward decline in trust, it is likely that we are simply witnessing a significant shift in the way that people choose to trust others – a move away from a deferential culture to one in which an informed public is more likely to challenge and critique institutions and professions.[9] The most important component of this shift is the general decline of trust in institutions. Organisations have traditionally provided a quick way for us to develop relationships with each other – in other words, I might trust a nurse because I trust the NHS. But the decline of institutional trust means that I have to assess the nurse as an individual before I can trust him or her. This clearly slows down the process of trust formation and makes it likely that we will trust fewer people overall.

There are some obvious drivers for these changing trust relationships – rising levels of individualism, a better educated citizenry, the increasing complexity of modern society, perhaps even a desire to appear 'streetwise'.[10] As this list suggests, a decline in trust may not be straightforwardly a bad thing – sceptical citizens seem likely to keep a close eye on their representatives. But when scepticism tips over into a generalised lack of trust in large and complex organisations like councils, the business of government becomes much more difficult, limiting the capacity of institutions to help the people they serve.

Regardless of whether or not there is a critical decline in levels of trust, our research clearly shows that developing more of it would have significant benefits for local government. These include fostering greater public willingness to engage with the council, greater confidence in its decisions and services, and greater public acceptance that 'mistakes happen' so long as they are acknowledged and rectified. At the national policy level, the benefits of devolving more power to local authorities can be realised only if council tax payers trust their representatives to use new powers in a responsible fashion.

The main policy approach to building trust over the past decade has been to improve services and reform governing structures to introduce executive mayors and cabinets. If there is an underlying model of trust building in the policies associated with the local government modernisation agenda, it is that service improvement, external accreditation and clearer governing structures will result in improved consumer experience, which will build trust.

But while there is plenty of evidence that services have improved, there is nothing to suggest that this has improved trust. In fact, satisfaction with local government – a closely related concept – has declined since 2000,[11] a problem that has been dubbed 'the performance paradox'. Local government has a persistent problem with the perceived fairness of its decisions.[12]

Our research provides a compelling explanation for this problem: trust is not built solely through services. At the institutional level, the public also takes into account the quality of personal interactions with council staff – particularly whether those interactions are emotionally satisfying.

The quality of a council's decision-making processes also matters, with the public demanding that local politicians make effective and fair choices about issues such as planning, regeneration and resource allocation. This is not just about the outcome of the decision, but the process by which it is taken – scrutiny matters as much as cabinet meetings.

The public is likely to trust a council only when they perceive it to be performing well against all three of these factors – services, interpersonal relations and decision making – although different groups of citizens will place much more emphasis on some trust factors than others.

This last fact is critical because, beyond the broad factors that make up institutional kinds of trust, different members of the public want very different relationships with their local authority. Citizens have a complex and sometimes emotionally charged relationship with local government, especially when they are depending on the council for basics like housing, or trusting it to administer tax collection or planning applications fairly. Different people use very different services, and therefore need to be able to delegate very different tasks to the council.

Our focus group work has allowed us to construct a broad but robust typology of these relationships, which are based largely on how dependent a particular member of the public is on their council (whether they are a 'have' or 'have not'), and the extent to which that member of the public thinks in an individualistic- or community-minded way (whether they are an 'I' or a 'we').

Broadly speaking, there are four kinds of relationship that the public wants with a council:

· **I haves:** Self-sufficient, busy and focused on work and entertainment, this group wants high levels of customer service on the rare occasions when they interact with the council.
· **I have nots:** Isolated and dependent, this group resents the fact that it needs public help for basics such as housing and benefits. They would like to be treated as consumers, but are frequently frustrated by the public sector's failure to meet their needs effectively.
· **We haves:** Wealthy activists who are often dedicated to improving the quality of their local area, this group has low

expectations for itself, but expects public services to improve the lives of others.

- **We have nots:** Housing estate activists who see collective action as a way to improve their lives, this group often sees itself as 'going into battle' with the council for a fair share of resources.

Trust-building strategies in local government need to be targeted at meeting the needs of these different groups. For instance, if a council wants to engage the public in decision making, it should probably start with the 'we' groups who are most interested in that realm of council activity, and then seek to ensure that those groups communicate effectively with the wider community about the decision-making process. Building trust also means accepting a degree of reciprocity in the relationship between the individual and the council – for instance, a council that wants the public to forgive its mistakes may have to extend the same courtesy to people who occasionally fail to make a tax or rent payment.

This report begins by seeking to define trust in a local government context, and examining key lessons from the literature on this topic. Chapter 3 then examines trust in the broad context of the government's public service reform agenda.

The remaining chapters draw on original research to show how trust can be better understood in practice, and how it can be developed. In chapter 4, we explore some of the key issues facing local government in terms of developing trust, including the role of service provision, staff attitudes and politics. Chapter 5 sets out a typology of different types of trust relationship and suggests three key areas that councils should focus on when building trust. Finally, chapters 6 and 7 analyse the practical implications of the research and set out the next steps for our work on trust in local government.

2 Defining trust

Trust is a slippery concept – entire books have been written to try and pin down its precise meaning, separating it from such related terms as 'esteem', 'satisfaction' and 'confidence'. Rather than enter this fraught theoretical debate, we began this project with a simple and practical dictionary definition of trust: 'Firm belief in the reliability, truth, ability or strength of someone or something.'

Trust is formed over time – it depends on multiple positive interactions between different parties. It is also intrinsically linked to behaviour: we can only really be said to trust someone when we are prepared to take a risk based on our assessment of their likely behaviour. As that suggests, we only need to trust in situations of uncertainty and where we are delegating a task to someone else.

So trust is ultimately a kind of gamble, a risky investment that we make every day to manage our lives in a complex and unpredictable world. It is also an emotionally charged investment, because to trust someone is to expose ourselves to the possibility of betrayal.

The alternative to trusting is either for us to disengage from a social relationship or to attempt to use fear, control and power to force the other party to behave in a way we find trustworthy. In the absence of trust, we have little choice but to resort to Machiavelli's unflattering argument that 'men have less hesitation in offending one who makes himself beloved than one who makes himself feared'.[13]

Trust is valuable because it facilitates cooperation and predictability, helping people work together and creating more effective relationships. The sociologist Barbara Mistzal offers a useful model that synthesises her discipline's views on the usefulness of trust (see figure 1).[14]

Figure 1   **Benefits of trust**

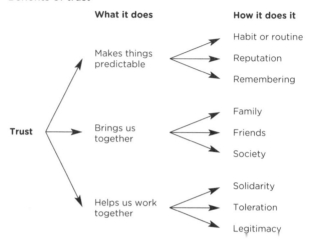

Source: Misztal, *Trust in Modern Societies.*

Trust formation – both between individuals and other individuals and between individuals and organisations – involves emotional and rational factors, and is conditioned by power relationships, personal attitudes and even someone's mood at any given time. When we asked focus group participants to define trust, they tended to do so in terms of the kind of behaviour they found trustworthy. The three most important themes to emerge for building personal trust were as follows:

· Trust has to be built as an ongoing, two-way relationship.
· It has to be based on honesty, reliability and regularity.
· It goes beyond the rational – there is an important emotional aspect.

Four additional factors came into play when the public was asked to trust a professional or service provider. These are all involved in establishing the competence of the professional:

· status reassurance – eg a qualification
· knowledgeability – demonstrated understanding of task
· expertise – ability to complete the task at hand
· word of mouth – recommendations from trusted sources can transfer trust to a professional

As this list suggests, institutions can also play an important role in creating a generalised kind of trust that helps us to put our faith in professionals who might often be strangers. By creating frameworks of rules and values, institutions are often able to bestow some degree of trustworthiness on their staff – we trust someone from the council because we think their membership of the organisation will lead them to behave in a broadly predictable way at a time when we need to delegate a task to them. More precisely, we might argue that institutions cannot be trusted per se, but that their value lies in their ability to create trustworthy rules, values and frameworks that help individuals form trusting relationships with each other.

The academic literature sets out two key approaches to developing trust, which might be described as *interest-* or *commitment-*based. The first tradition argues that service providers are essentially self-interested, but can be trusted when there are specific incentives in place for them to act in the consumer's interest, perhaps including profit or the threat of sanctions for poor performance. This way of thinking about trust prioritises the importance of institutions and structures in ensuring that the interests of service providers and consumers are aligned. The second tradition emphasises the commitment and intrinsic motivations of service providers. In other words, it suggests that we are likely to trust people when we believe that they are sufficiently motivated by goodwill to help us.[15]

Of course, these views can easily be synthesised. Our research suggests that there can in fact be a circular relationship between institutional attempts to align the interests of staff and customers, and the intrinsic goodwill of workers themselves. The fact that my local council appears to have robust and trustworthy rules and systems will make me more likely to trust its staff, but only if those staff also behave in a trustworthy way consistent with their employer's stated values. The key is to create a trusted institutional framework that still leaves plenty of room for individuals to express goodwill and initiative.

If staff behave badly, then that seems likely to reduce the amount of trust I place in their employer, and if the council behaves badly, I am less likely to trust staff, or I might decide that the staff are trustworthy despite their employer. In practical terms, this kind of institutional trust can be built only if the public finds the rules and values attractive, and if those values are reflected in day-to-day interactions between staff and the public.[16]

This helps to explain why teachers and doctors remain so highly trusted. They work within strong institutional constraints symbolised by their professional qualifications, they are subject to heavy regulation and are often assumed to be motivated by a set of caring values. If they fail to live up to professional standards, they are heavily penalised. The rules and values associated with their employers and professional background help us feel that we can predict their actions to the extent that we will gladly entrust our children's safety to them. They effectively combine institutional and personal and interest- and commitment-based forms of trust.

Beyond this general approach to building trust in organisations, there are a number of key issues that specifically affect politicians and political institutions.

Political trust

Politics lies at the heart of public institutions and if politicians and their decisions are not trusted, our research suggests that the public's trust in the council as a whole is reduced. There are at least two key approaches to building trust in political systems: one which focuses on institutions and formal processes, and another which focuses on personalities, performance and informal processes. The first would emphasise the importance of constitutional changes such as House of Lords reform, while the latter would focus on the trustworthiness of individual politicians.

Increasing trust in politics probably means acting on both of these fronts simultaneously. The public seems unlikely to love either a good system run by untrustworthy politicians, or good politicians who allow an unfair system to remain in place.

Institutional factors are important because research shows that people will often accept negative outcomes if they believe that the decision-making process was carried out in a fair way. This dynamic has been demonstrated in a range of settings, including the legal system, performance-related pay at work and interactions with the police.[17]

One study presents six key criteria for establishing this kind of 'procedural fairness':[18]

· consistency – equal treatment across people and time
· bias suppression – the avoidance of personal interest and ideological bias by public officials
· accuracy – utilising up-to-date, accurate information and opinion
· correctability – the provision of opportunity for review, appeal or redress
· representativeness – ensuring that all citizens can be involved in decision making or that a representative view has been taken
· ethics – decisions must conform to fundamental moral values

We need to be equally concerned with the practice and personalities of politics. Numerous studies have highlighted the importance of political performance in building trust – making the basic point that representatives will gain trust if they deliver desirable results and keep their promises.

In local government, work from the Standards Board for England highlights the importance of performance alongside the need to keep closely in touch with local needs and preferences. In a national survey, the board found that the top four kinds of behaviour the public expects from councillors are:[19]

· making sure public money is spent wisely
· being in touch with what the public thinks is important

- doing what they promised when elected
- working in the interests of the neighbourhood

It is worth noting that the public is sceptical about the extent to which their councillors actually exhibit this behaviour in practice. A majority of those surveyed for the Standards Board study believed that councillors did not display the first three types of behaviour listed above.

Inequality and trust

Income inequality appears to be one of the most important factors in undermining political trust.[20] Our research suggests that this is at least partly because the poor resent their dependence on public services – they are effectively forced to trust local government or to go without essential services – while the wealthy may in some cases resent paying for services they rarely use.

The importance of inequality can also be seen at the level of individual trust decisions. Lower status groups worry that if they trust another person or organisation, they may ultimately lose out financially. Encouraging trust among these groups is likely to involve reducing risk, offering insurance mechanisms or compensation for when things go wrong.

By contrast, high status groups are less worried about potential financial losses and more worried about the potential for betrayal. The key goal for these groups is to reduce the likelihood of that betrayal, for instance through incentives for service providers to behave in a trustworthy fashion.[21]

Institutions and trust

People find it far easier to trust individuals than institutions. For instance, while 91 per cent of the British public would trust a doctor to tell the truth, only 71 per cent would trust the NHS as a whole.[22] As this suggests, people appear to draw a distinction between the individual representing the organisation, and the behaviour of the organisation itself.

Public institutions are often seen to be dominated by 'managers' and 'bureaucrats' who counterbalance the good work of frontline staff. Some people have developed a generalised lack of trust in large organisations per se, not trusting 'the system' despite some positive personal interactions.[23]

This is particularly true when an institution is seen as being removed from the daily concerns of ordinary people. Ipsos MORI has identified a strong correlation between perceptions of remoteness and of value for money – in other words, it has identified that the more remote people feel the council is, the less cost-effective they believe it to be. The notion that remoteness breeds contempt is borne out by a wealth of survey data showing that the public tends to place more trust in people they deal with personally – local councillors, for instance, are consistently thought to be more trustworthy than MPs.[24]

More prosaically, it seems that the larger the population of a city, the lower the levels of trust in its local government institutions.[25]

Emotional and rational trust

It is increasingly recognised that trust is composed of both rational and emotional – or *cognitive* and *affective* – elements.[26] Both of these factors need to be present to generate genuinely trusting relationships between service providers and the public. Cognitive trust relates to someone's willingness to depend on a service provider's competence and reliability. These judgements are based on knowledge accumulated either through personal experience of a service provider, or through word of mouth and reputation.

Affective trust is based on the feeling of care and concern that a person feels when dealing with a service provider. It leads to people feeling that they have developed secure and strong relationships. This kind of trust is often based on a feeling that a service provider is intrinsically motivated to provide a good service – like the apparently vocational motivation of many doctors and teachers.

People's recollection of their past trust experiences seems to be based primarily on two factors – the peak emotional experience and the outcome of the interaction.[27] The duration of the experience does not seem to matter a great deal. The implication for public servants is that quick service and a good outcome will not build trust if the service experience is frustrating or depressing for the user. From a trust perspective, it is better to take longer if you can use the time to deliver a better emotional experience.

The way we approach trust relationships may even be affected by our mood – with people who are feeling happy being more likely to take decisions based on past experiences, and those who are unhappy being more critical of their current situation.

An ideal trust relationship?

Some writers suggest that ideal trust relationships can be formed only through repeated interactions in relatively small groups. These interactions are likely to build more trust within the group, and also to make members of the group more trustworthy in general. In other words, members of small partnership groups are likely to be more trustworthy even when interacting with people outside the group.[28]

Game theory experiments suggest that people are generally 'conditional cooperators' – in other words, we are most prepared to trust others and work together if we believe that other people's intentions are fair, that free riders will be penalised, and that cooperators will be rewarded.[29] Cooperation can be encouraged by:

· being aware of the future because cooperation is generally a more beneficial and predictable strategy in the long term
· changing the payoffs and ensure that non-cooperation is heavily penalised
· teaching people to care about the welfare of others
· teaching people about the benefits of reciprocity
· encouraging people to recognise the patterns of other people's responses to sustain long run cooperation[30]

Taken together, these factors suggest that councils need to encourage what the social scientist Robert Sampson calls *collective efficacy* – the idea that members of the public are more likely to take action on issues like truancy if they believe that others are doing the same.[31] By creating positive experiences of collective action and demonstrating palpable benefits from that action, councils may be able to generate the conditions for long-term trust and collaboration among communities. In doing so, they may be able to generate more sustainable policy solutions that help members of the community rely on each other rather than the council.

3 Trust and public service reform

Perhaps the most challenging lesson from the literature is the fact that service improvement is not in itself enough to build trust. This is recognised to varying degrees among the councils we worked with. Some senior officers saw trust and higher performance as largely interchangeable, but others anticipated our findings by identifying broader factors. For instance, Lewisham's chief executive, Barry Quirk, commented that: 'Improving trust means going beyond the first order issue of services and thinking about how we make decisions.'[32]

There are a number of reasons why service improvement is not enough. For, instance, it might be that the public and the government have different views of what constitutes improvement. Many people use only a small number of public services and they tend to be more favourable about those of which they have direct experience. The public often does not understand which agency delivers what service, and may not consider all public services to be 'public'.

Some services will feature much more powerfully in their imagination than others – everyone has an interest in clean streets, but only a minority of us have direct experience of social care. It is for precisely this reason that the Local Government Association's campaign to improve the reputation of councils focuses on 'cleaner, safer and greener' areas and better communications.[33] Perhaps most importantly, objective performance is not the only criterion that people use to evaluate government – expectations, perceptions and socio-economic factors all have an impact on satisfaction.[34]

These factors have led to a situation in the UK in which many people admit to having positive personal interactions with public services, but consider the public sector as a whole to be performing poorly – the so-called 'performance paradox' in which services improve, but satisfaction falls. In local government, scores for single- and upper-tier councils in the Comprehensive Performance Assessment (CPA) rose significantly between 2003 and 2006 – the number of 'good' and 'excellent' performers rising from 55 per cent to 78 per cent – but average satisfaction scores have declined from 53 per cent to 51 per cent over the same period.[35]

Low levels of trust may go some way towards explaining this situation – a member of the public might have had a good experience of a local government service, but attribute this to the individual providing that service rather than trusting the institution to provide consistent high standards.

This situation is compounded by what the political scientist Peter Taylor-Gooby terms 'the efficiency/trust dilemma'.[36] The government's approach to public service reform has been heavily influenced by the new public management and principal–agent theory, both of which see individuals as fundamentally self-interested, and therefore emphasise the importance of targets, incentives and punishments as a way to force public servants to behave in the interests of consumers.

This approach appeals to our rational minds by improving the efficacy of public service provision, but Taylor-Gooby's research suggests that it may also send a message that public servants are basically selfish and not to be trusted. In so doing, it seems to actually undermine the emotional elements of the trust relationship – which our research suggests are heavily dependent on a sense of public service values and intrinsic motivation.

This is played out daily in local and national performance management regimes, which routinely limit the amount of discretion professionals and customer contact staff have to deal with citizens. The effect is to limit the space for conversation and negotiation at the frontline, which many researchers and analysts argue is critical for developing trusting relationships.[37]

Building trust requires the existence of a shared space where individuals can engage in a reciprocal dialogue to negotiate a shared outcome, beyond the general predefined limits of their role as 'council staff' and 'council client'. Within the contexts of councils, trust requires an investment of time in 'clients' and the delegation of autonomy and decision-making capability to staff.

None of this is to suggest that service improvement is not important – many international studies identify 'performance' as the most significant constituent of trust in government.[38] It is simply to argue that we need to interpret the idea of performance broadly – recognising that higher standards matter only if they result in better experiences by the public.

4 Local government in context

Local authorities can find themselves in a challenging position – assailed by rising levels of inequality and diversity, poorly understood by the public and seen as just one small part of the broader system of government. In these circumstances, it is perhaps not surprising that councils often fail to build effective, two-way relationships with their citizens. The problem is compounded by staff who are often more concerned with trust issues within the local authority than with using trust as a way of building relationships with the public. The net result can be citizens who resent their dependence on local government.

But councils also appear to have some distinct advantages in terms of trust development. Compared with other parts of government, they are closer to people and have opportunities to interact with the public relatively frequently. This means that even when they do not have close relationships with citizens, they are in a reasonably good position to build them.

The public remains deeply attached to the ideals and goals of public service and local governance, even if they do not always like the reality. As MORI found in a 2004 survey: 'People have a dream of locally based, locally accountable institutions, even if the reality never quite lives up to this.'[39]

This was confirmed by our own research with members of the public and council staff, as well as a wealth of polling data which shows that citizens are more likely to trust people who seem local and accountable over those who do not – one survey found that 48 per cent trust their local MP, but only 29 per cent trust MPs in general and fewer still trust ministers.[40]

Perhaps most importantly, our research shows that local government also has a large degree of control over the most important factors in developing trust – personal experience and word of mouth.

Key research findings in this section include the following:

- **There are significant benefits to being trusted.** These include a greater public willingness to engage with local government, greater confidence in service delivery and decision making, and more willingness to forgive council mistakes.
- **Councils are failing to build good relationships.** Trust is based on an ongoing, two-way relationship, but for most people in most council areas this is not present. This problem is complicated by the fact that most people did not know what their council did or who their councillor was.
- **Most public interactions are about negative issues.** People often make contact with the council only when something goes wrong, meaning that their interaction was usually only about negative issues. Some councillors compound this problem by actively seeking complaints.
- **Trust works differently in the public sector.** The public trusts businesses very differently from the way it trusts councils. Public servants are perceived to be motivated by a degree of goodwill and a desire to help, while businesses are trusted because they offer people the choice to exit and go elsewhere if things go wrong.

The value of trust

Almost all local government services require some basic level of trust. For instance, the public is unlikely to sort its waste if people do not believe the council will recycle it effectively. Our focus group participants identified five key benefits of increasing trust above this basic level:

- Willingness to engage: Trust potentially leads to higher election turnouts and participation in consultations.
- Greater confidence in decision making: People are more likely to trust the council to make the best decision.
- Greater willingness to accept 'unwanted' decisions: Trust leads people to be less critical of unfavourable outcomes.

- Greater confidence in service delivery: People are more willing to believe that things will happen as promised.
- Forgiveness of mistakes: People are more likely to accept failure if they trust that the council was doing its best.

Service relationships

When you call up [the council] you never know who you are speaking to and you often get the feeling they don't know what they are doing anyway.
Female, 35–44, BC1, Lewisham

The most common service delivery problem among our four councils was their failure to build ongoing relationships with individual members of the public. Most people in our focus groups had experienced very little personal interaction with their local authority. Interactions tended to be about one-off problems, with members of the public rarely speaking to the same person twice. This creates a sense that councils are 'faceless'. Postal communications are no more effective, with most ignored due to 'boring design'. The public in our four areas generally remembered only election manifestos and council tax bills. Once again, these findings are consistent with other qualitative studies of public interactions with local government.[41]

So public interactions with a council are usually framed in negative terms from the start – you speak to the council only when you have a problem, and when you do contact them you are dealing with a faceless organisation where no one seems to be on your side.

This was a particular problem for those members of the public who were economically disadvantaged and therefore dependent on the council for crucial services. These groups often felt that they had very clear needs that the local authority should be meeting, but that staff in the council failed to understand and appreciate the urgency of those needs. For instance, one focus group participant told us how she contacted the local authority because a window frame in her council house was rotting, only to be told that it was not yet rotten enough to warrant replacement. Her response was to spray the window with water every day to make it rot faster. Situations like this can leave disadvantaged citizens feeling angry, impotent and frustrated – an emotional response that is often met with defensiveness from council staff.

This is exacerbated by the lack of contact that the public has with middle managers within councils. These are often the people who have the most power to respond to customer concerns – one reason why frontline staff and middle managers account for the majority of innovations in the public sectors of developed Commonwealth countries[42] – and yet the public often speaks to them only to resolve a particularly troubling complaint.

Focus group participants were often well informed about their council's use of formal partnerships – for instance those in social housing usually knew whether their landlord was a housing association, local authority or ALMO (arm's length management organisation). Housing is clearly a special case as the landlord–tenant relationship is so powerful, but some participants could identify other visible services such as refuse collection that were delivered by the private sector. However, they still held the council responsible for quality and performance, and were liable to blame service failure on the council regardless of whether the service was in-house or outsourced.

Political relationships

Focus group participants generally said that they had very little contact with their councillors and few could identify their own representative – a finding that is echoed by national surveys showing that just a third of people claim to know the name of a local councillor.[43] Most participants knew very little about what councillors do apart from a vague sense that they were 'decision makers'.[44] One focus group participant in Lewisham argued that 'the average Joe never gets to see these people'.

This is concerning because councillors are the main formal link between the citizen and the decision-making process – if people have no contact with their councillor, they are unlikely to be able to develop a trusting relationship with the decision-making process. It seems likely that developing higher visibility for ward councillors is the necessary first step towards developing real community leadership in local government.

Wakefield and rural parts of Sunderland were exceptions to this rule, with relatively high levels of recognition for local councillors. Lewisham's directly elected mayor also had unusually high levels of name recognition, although there was no evidence to suggest that this resulted in greater trust for the council. When asked if they knew who the mayor of Lewisham was, many people confused the council's executive mayor, Steve Bullock, with the then London mayor, Ken Livingstone.

The councillors we spoke to took very different views of the quality of their own engagement with the public. Some argued that they were already part of their community, that they spoke to their constituents all the time in the course of their daily lives and that they therefore had little reason to change their behaviour.

A second group, often in opposition, was fatalistic about the decline of public interest in their work. They sometimes blamed the media for this. One councillor in Solihull argued that the public was less likely to come to them with problems because of improvements in the council's customer contact centre, which meant it was easier to resolve issues over the phone with an official. Some councillors argued that the introduction of executives had reduced the role and importance of backbenchers.

A third and final group recognised the problem of public disengagement and was enthusiastic about neighbourhood governance arrangements as a way to re-engage with the public.

As this suggests, some councillors saw their relationship with the public as a series of one-off problem-solving engagements. There had sometimes been little attempt to build longer-term relationships with constituents around more positive decisions, although councillors were beginning to experiment with this approach. The public seems likely to welcome a more proactive style of politics – focus group research shows that people want their councillors to be down to earth, approachable, available and good listeners who can get things done.[45]

Finally, 'politics' may itself be a factor in undermining trust in the council. Opposition councillors all wanted to be trusted to take on power, but their campaigns often aimed at undermining trust in the ruling group and the council as a whole. Successful opposition campaigns might actually undermine the institutions that politicians seek to run.

The staff view

When we asked council staff to define the benefits of trust, they usually did so in terms of whether or not they felt personally trusted by their colleagues and managers. Frontline groups felt that being trusted at work was important for their own confidence, self-esteem and morale. A minority of frontline staff, particularly those in Lewisham and Sunderland, argued that being trusted by the public would allow them to get more honest information from the residents they served, and create an environment in which they could take risks and innovate.

Middle managers tended to see trust as an organisational issue, arguing that if their staff trusted them, they would be better able to create process change, increase organisational adaptability, take informed risks and improve their organisational efficiency.

Underlying both sets of responses was an understanding that within a trusting environment people feel confident to give and accept criticism, they are able to make changes quickly, ideas can be tested robustly, and creativity and individuality can be expressed. The staff responses seemed to imply that public servants see themselves as part of a 'chain of trust' – in other words, that staff could build trusting relationships with the public only if they were trusted by their own managers and co-workers.

Council staff generally felt that they were personally trusted by the people they served. Frontline staff felt that trust depended on their performance, while middle managers tended to see it as a function of their relationships with other people within the council and with key external partners. Perhaps paradoxically, neither group was prepared to be very trusting of others, often complaining that members of the public were not honest enough, or that their colleagues did not work to a high enough standard.

Staff felt that council services were trusted provided that:

· staff were able to deliver as promised
· the client had realistic expectations
· staff were able to communicate effectively
· the client did not have negative preconceptions

But staff gave considerably more nuanced answers to the question of whether the public trusted the council as an institution. Some frontline staff felt that 'there was no council to trust'. Instead of being a single tangible entity, the council was seen more as a collection of services and individuals. In this context, it was argued that the public could not trust 'the council', especially as standards would vary from department to department.

This suggests that the fragmentation of local government into a variety of partnerships may make trust building more difficult, as it makes it harder to project a coherent set of organisational rules and values to the public.

Local government as part of 'the system'

The process of trust building is complicated by the fact that members of the public taking part in our focus groups tended to see councils as a small and relatively unimportant part of the broader system of government. Perceptions of a council are therefore heavily influenced by perceptions of 'the government' as a whole – particularly a sense of an overly protective, nannying state. As one participant from Solihull put it: 'Why should we trust them when all they do is slow things down and make our lives more difficult?'

The way that focus group participants viewed the council was also heavily influenced by the performance of other, higher-profile local services such as the NHS and police. This is partly a reflection of the fact that the focus groups placed relatively little importance on the services provided by the council – they assume it deals with relatively trivial matters, they do not link together the wide range of services councils provide, and they assume that central government has a greater impact on their lives.

A general lack of contact with the council means that the public's decisions on whether to trust their local authority are based on limited information about the institution's performance, services and purpose, a finding confirmed by other qualitative studies.[46] In the absence of an ongoing relationship, three principal factors matter in building trust (see figure 2). Personal experience matters most because it is direct. It is most often related to particular services or to bills and payments, and most people could cite an experience of service failure.

Word of mouth is the second most influential factor, with all participants knowing someone who had experienced bad service. Many council staff felt that the media had a particularly negative impact on trust, but our research suggests that it is in fact only the third most influential factor.

Figure 2   **How people decide to trust the council**

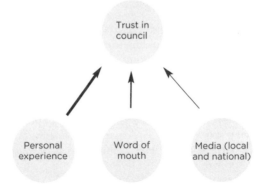

Public service values and the problem of dependency

People tend to form different kinds of trust relationships with the public and private sectors. Their assumption is often that public professionals such as doctors and teachers are intrinsically motivated to help citizens, and that while public servants cannot always deliver good results, they are generally doing their best in difficult circumstances. The downside of this is that the public sometimes feels that it has no choice but to trust local government, and this can create feelings of dependency and resentment. In contrast, private businesses were seen to be trustworthy largely because they had lots of incentives to provide good customer service – businesses treat people well because they want their custom.

We asked council staff to discuss whether they trusted a range of organisations from the public, private and voluntary sectors. Some important distinctions emerged that were echoed in our research with members of the public.

Council staff frequently saw the profit motive itself as part of a negative business agenda – suggesting that it often led to organisations caring more about sales than people. This suspicion could be cancelled out if businesses delivered consistently high standards of service and mechanisms to reduce the risk of something going wrong. The most trusted private sector companies like Marks & Spencer were seen to provide consistently high levels of quality and to reduce the risk of shopping through a 'no questions' return policy.

The public sector trust dynamic is very different. While staff tended to trust organisations like the NHS and their own council, they argued that in many cases they had no choice but to do so, because they were dependent on a monopoly public sector supplier. What made this acceptable were the values that lay behind councils and hospitals. Staff often argued that these institutions were broadly on their side and did not deliberately seek to frustrate or cheat them. As one middle manager in Lewisham argued when talking about his own council: 'I trust them, but they're not always very good… they don't deliberately give you a hard time.'

The implication is that people may be more prepared to forgive occasional errors in a public service because they sympathise with an idealised vision of the aims of the organisation. But when public services fail to live up to their values, the dependency relationship becomes deeply problematic. The participants in our focus groups who were angriest were those who could not get the help they needed and deeply resented having to rely on the council for support. The dependency relationship can create a close bond between a council and its citizens, but if it sours it can be corrosive of trust. It needs to be managed very carefully.

Trust and communities

Trust relationships between councils and their citizens are often shaped by specifically local historical, economic and social factors.

For instance, we found that low trust in Sunderland council was deeply related to the area's economic decline and the resented sense of dependency this had created among the community. While there was strong social trust among communities in the area, this had been formed through adversity and there was a sense of solidarity in opposition to the council.

Wakefield council has developed a more positive trust relationship partly because of the strong social capital legacy of its industrial past. The community appeared to feel that many of its social problems were not the council's fault, but were caused by particular 'problem people', and that it was the community's job to deal with these people.

At the other end of the scale, people in Lewisham tended to have unrealistic expectations of the council's power to deal with collective problems like anti-social behaviour. This might suggest that strong social capital is likely to create more capable communities, which will in turn have greater capacity to deal with their own social problems without public sector help.

People in every area we visited believed that levels of trust were declining in their local community, largely due to broad trends such as the decline of high streets, a lack of organised communal activities, a career- and money-focused culture and a media-fostered climate of fear about crime.

5 Trust in local government

If I trusted them to do it, I wouldn't feel so annoyed with them when things go wrong... also if I believed they made the best decisions it wouldn't be so bad.
Male, 25–34, BC1, Sunderland

There are significant opportunities for councils to develop a higher trust relationship with their citizens, but doing so in practice requires a more detailed understanding of exactly what factors the public takes into account when deciding to trust or not. If service improvement is not enough, then what else is necessary?

Our research found that there are three different factors involved in building trust with the council as an organisation. These factors are additive – in other words trust in the council as a whole emerges only when all of them are present. The first is the quality of people's personal interactions, or their trust in the people providing services directly. The second is trust in services, judged on the visible outcomes of the service. The final factor is decision making, or trust in the council's capacity to make fair choices about policy and spending. These factors are explained in more detail below.

This formula provides a compelling explanation for the 'performance paradox'. The many councils that combine apparently high CPA performance with low levels of trust and satisfaction may be delivering good services, but failing to provide consistently good personal service to citizens or to build trust in their decision-making processes.

But it is important to note that not everyone wants the same relationship with the council, and different groups of people will emphasise different aspects of trust – some will be more interested in personal service, while others will care about decision making. In order to analyse these different relationships, this chapter sets out an original typology of four different kinds of 'truster' identified through our focus group research.

By combining this typology with our new understanding of how to build trust in local government, we are able to present a number of strategies for developing more trusting relationships with these different groups.

Our key findings in this chapter include that:

- **Improving services is not enough.** Better services do not necessarily 'spill over' into broader trust in the council, even when combined with good personal service.
- **Fairness matters.** Decision making is a key area of weakness for local government, with decision makers often seen as remote and out of touch. One reason for this is the failure of many authorities to communicate their decisions in a way that impacts on people's everyday lives. There was a particular concern with the 'fairness' of decision making in all council areas.
- **Politicians have a key role to play in building trust.** Councillors have the potential to bridge the gap between personal and decision-making forms of trust, but this will require a much more active and involved local politics, with far more face-to-face contact between politicians and the public and a significant change in the public's perceptions of councillor activities.

Below, we set out the three key types of trust that councils need to develop.

Trust in people, services and decisions
Personal interactions

This kind of trust grows out of positive interactions between citizens and individual frontline staff, usually in the context of delivering a service. Key players in building this kind of trust are likely to include call centre operatives, social workers, teachers and neighbourhood wardens.

Trust in individual members of staff is built using the same model of professional trust outlined above – in other words status reassurance, demonstrated knowledgeability and expertise are critical. In addition, the public expects staff to be honest, reliable and friendly. Ideally, staff would also show empathy, care and integrity.

Service delivery and recovery
Trust in services is based on the public's overall perception of their quality. Good services often require little personal interaction with citizens, so the public tends to judge their quality on the basis of visible and personally relevant services, typically including:

· clean streets
· street lighting
· refuse collection and recycling
· billing processes
· personal benefits from services such as education and social care

When people did interact with these services, they expected their request to be dealt with professionally and to be acted on in good time. Councils also needed to become better at recovering the situation when things went wrong, admitting mistakes and making amends.

Decision making
The public also judges councils based on their perceived competence in making decisions that affect the whole local area – often including issues like planning, regeneration and allocating budgets. The public's overarching concern was that decisions should be 'fair', but because they have little understanding of the way that councils take decisions they generally make this judgement based on media reports and personal experience, for instance of seeing the results of successful regeneration projects. This is not just a problem for the four councils in our sample – the Lyons Inquiry found that it was a general issue across local government.[47]

It would be a mistake to see trust in decision making as

something built only in cabinet meetings. People's perceptions of decisions, and of their fairness, seem likely to be formed by a wider range of factors, including a sense that their voice and opinion was heard and a sense that the decision was subjected to strong scrutiny. This means that the way a decision is communicated, discussed and scrutinised by backbenchers may be at least as important as the outcome of that decision.

The factors that matter most for building decision-making trust are:

- planning
- service strategy
- spending decisions
- economic and social development

People who trusted the council as a decision maker had often had positive experiences of the planning system, or had witnessed the successful development of their area.

Relationships between different aspects of trust

The model we have set out above goes a long way to explaining the performance paradox. A council that is delivering good services and therefore hitting its performance indicators and scoring well on its inspections might simultaneously be delivering inconsistent customer service and failing to build trust in its decision-making functions. Anecdotal evidence suggests that some councils are in fact currently grappling with this problem.

While our research suggests that there is a reasonably strong relationship between personal and service levels of trust, it is much less clear that building trust in these areas creates a 'spill-over' effect into trust in the council as a decision-making body. In other words, the public may feel that they are receiving a good service despite the fact that 'the system' as a whole is broken.

So efforts to build trust in people and services are likely to be mutually reinforcing, but there is a much weaker link between

Figure 3   **How different kinds of trust interact**

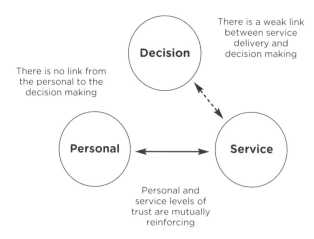

services and decision making, and almost no link between trust in people and trust in decision making (see figure 3).

The reason for this disconnect between people and decision-making forms of trust seems clear – few people ever have the chance to interact with the councillors and senior officers involved in the decision-making process. Our focus groups generally had a poor understanding of the strategic and political functions of their local authority, and few participants knew or cared about their councillors. Even councils that have introduced measures for decision-making transparency – such as Lewisham's public mayor and cabinet meetings – are not immune from this sense that decision making is becoming detached from people's everyday lives.

The single biggest priority for local government as it moves into a place-shaping role may therefore be to develop a better understanding of how local people judge 'fairness'; to reflect that understanding in the visible impact of their decisions; and ultimately to create better links between the decision-making process and personal trust relationships. As representatives and decision makers, councillors seem the obvious people to bridge this divide between the personal and political.

Four ways of seeing trust

The obvious objection to such a strategy is that the public shows little sign of being interested in decision-making processes, and that lack of trust in those processes is therefore inevitable. Our research indicates that this is not quite true. Different groups of citizens form their trust judgements in different ways, placing varying degrees of emphasis on the three different building blocks of trust. Some sections of the population base their trust judgements very heavily on the council's decision-making capacity.

Many of the factors we might usually expect to predict trust relationships do not hold good in relation to the public sector – for instance age and class are poor predictors of whether someone is likely to trust their council or not.[48] So one of the key goals of our research work was to develop our understanding of the kind of trust relationship that the public wants to form with their council. To that end, we used our focus groups with members of the public to create an empirical typology of different kinds of 'truster'.

Two key factors structure the relationships that members of the public want with local government. First is the extent of a person's dependency on the council – in other words, are they a 'have' or a 'have not'? Second is the degree to which people have an individualistic or community-spirited mindset, or whether they are a 'we' or a 'me':

· **Haves** tend to be self-sufficient, with adequate incomes and living in private owned or rented accommodation.
· **Have nots** tend to be dependent on the council, often on income support and typically live in social housing.
· **I thinkers** tend to focus on personal needs and development, and to be competitive in outlook.
· **We thinkers** tend to be community-focused and collective in outlook.

Figure 4   **Truster types**

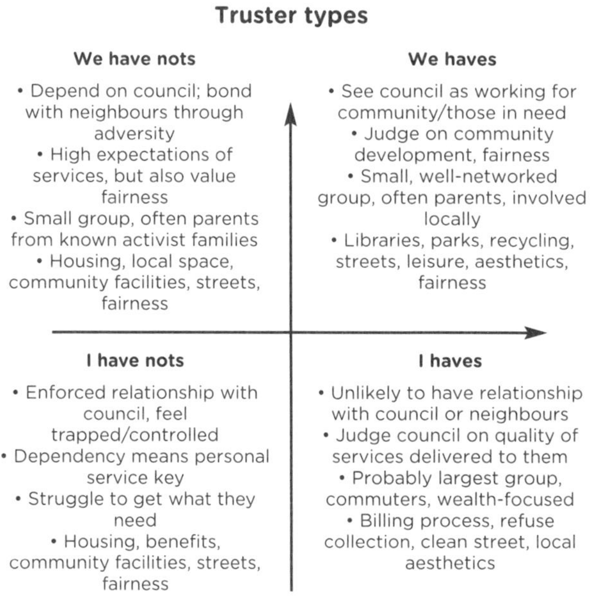

Truster types

We have nots	We haves
• Depend on council; bond with neighbours through adversity • High expectations of services, but also value fairness • Small group, often parents from known activist families • Housing, local space, community facilities, streets, fairness	• See council as working for community/those in need • Judge on community development, fairness • Small, well-networked group, often parents, involved locally • Libraries, parks, recycling, streets, leisure, aesthetics, fairness
I have nots	**I haves**
• Enforced relationship with council, feel trapped/controlled • Dependency means personal service key • Struggle to get what they need • Housing, benefits, community facilities, streets, fairness	• Unlikely to have relationship with council or neighbours • Judge council on quality of services delivered to them • Probably largest group, commuters, wealth-focused • Billing process, refuse collection, clean street, local aesthetics

These four factors create four broad kinds of trust relationship between the citizen and the council. We saw examples of all four relationships in each of the council areas we visited. Each group needs to delegate very different tasks to the local authority, so councils will need to develop distinctive strategies for building trust with different types. The four types are described in detail in figure 4.

We haves make up a relatively small proportion of our focus group sample, but it seems likely that they are one of the most socially networked and therefore influential groups in our typology. They typically had spare time and a desire to be proactive about local social issues. Many of them are parents who have built up strong social capital through their concern for their children – for instance through getting involved in local schools. Some members of this type become more active once their children leave home.

This group of affluent activists tends to be well informed about local issues, particularly from reading the local press. They would like to be treated as service consumers, but have low personal expectations. They do expect the council to help deliver community development through fair service provision and spending decisions.

While this group is prepared to interact with the council to get things done, they often get frustrated with public service institutions, seeing them as unsupportive or nannying.

We have nots were also a relatively small group, but they wielded a significant amount of influence on their neighbourhood. They generally live in social housing, creating strong bonds with their neighbours through shared adversity. Often from a well-known family of community organisers, they tend to have time to spare and a proactive attitude. This group also contains many parents.

The 'we have nots' are less altruistic than their wealthy counterparts. They often have individual problems with council services, particularly benefits and housing, but feel that the best way to resolve those problems is through community action and strength in numbers. This group likens civic activism to 'going into battle' to secure the things they feel they deserve and are entitled to.

I haves are probably the largest of the four groups. They are self-sufficient, lead busy lifestyles and are focused on work and entertainment. Most young people fall into this category – they tend to be living in a particular area due to financial constraints rather than personal choice, to be highly mobile and to make greater use of 'virtual communities' through the internet. The result is that they seldom integrate into their neighbourhoods. This group wants to be treated as consumers of council services, which they see as important to 'keep things working'.

I have nots are usually isolated from the community around them and dependent on the council for financial or social support. They often feel that they cannot help themselves and so they struggle with the council to get the support they believe they are entitled to. Many resent their dependency and feel trapped or controlled by public agencies. Housing and benefits are key services for this group, although many of them also have specific personal needs. They would like to be treated as consumers of council services, but are often frustrated with the failure of local institutions to meet their needs quickly and effectively.

6 Strategies for building trust

The ideal trust relationship is built through a combination of trust in a council's individual staff, service delivery and decision-making capacity, but different groups of citizens want different kinds of relationships with the council, placing different emphasis on personal, service and decision-making levels of trust. This reflects the fact that different groups are concerned with delegating different tasks to the council.

For instance, the consumerist 'I haves' are primarily interested in the quality of the services they personally receive, so the starting point for building trust with this group is improving the quality of customer service and delivering good visible service outcomes. Conversely, this group is unlikely to pay a great deal of attention to decision-making structures and procedures. It may be that the only way to persuade this group to become more interested in governance issues is to convert them into 'we haves', perhaps through developing their usage of community facilities, creating opportunities for them to collaborate in community projects in areas like crime and the local environment, and encouraging voluntary sector activity in wealthier areas.

This clearly has implications for a number of local government services. For instance, a council that wants to engage more effectively with citizens might want to consider face-to-face neighbourhood management to help the 'I have nots' access services and solve their problems, linking them to sources of help from all sectors across the area. The 'I haves' are highly mobile and might be best reached through the internet, particularly if councils can find innovative ways to involve this group in taking decisions online.

Figure 5 sets out which groups are most interested in which areas of trust.

Figure 5 **How different types trust**

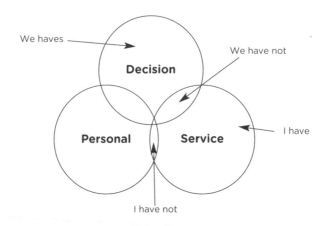

The interests of different groups can be explained partly by the very different needs of different truster types. The 'I have nots', for instance, often rely on the public sector for the basics of a decent existence, including money and housing. What they get and the degree to which they are allowed to receive it in a dignified way matters a great deal.

By way of contrast, the 'we haves' are often people who have met their own personal needs and are now looking to the outside world for fulfilment or as a means to achieve broad social goals. This might be because they want to live in a nicer area, and realise that this can be done only through collective action, or it may reflect a genuine concern with the needs of others.

By understanding which groups are most interested in which areas of trust building, we can identify the issues which areas councils should focus on as the starting point for building trust with different groups.

We haves have few expectations of the council for themselves, but a great deal of interest in the way its decisions affect the local environment, other people and the common good. Building trust for this group means involving them in decisions about planning and economic and social regeneration, as well as providing aid and support for the community projects that many of this group are involved with.

Key trust factors for this group include:

· recycling
· street cleaning
· education
· appearance of the local area
· amenities such as leisure centres, parks, libraries
· fairness in decision making
· community-building initiatives
· developing the local economy

We have nots are mainly concerned with improving their own local services and local environment, so this group's key interests lie in the way decisions improve their lives and those of the people who live around them. Building trust for this group is likely to mean involving them in decisions about their own community, using them as sounding boards for community feeling and encouraging self-help schemes that reduce community dependence on the council. Their strong concern with the fairness of spending decisions means it may also be valuable to involve them in budget allocation so they understand the basis of council decisions.

Key trust factors for this group are the performance of housing and community services – the quality of their local environment, facilities for young people and children and the provision of amenities such as leisure centres all feature highly. In decision-making terms, they are highly concerned to ensure that they and their community receive a 'fair' share of spending.

I haves are almost exclusively concerned with the quality of the services that they use personally. To the extent that councils can build trust with this largely disengaged group, they can do so through improving the quality of a handful of key services and highlighting the value that the council brings to the local area – helping the 'I haves' to understand where their money goes.

Key services for this group are:

- billing processes
- refuse collection
- clean streets
- local aesthetics
- parks

The only way to build a deeper and more trusting relationship with this group is probably to try and shift them into becoming 'we' thinkers.

I have nots might be described as 'frustrated consumers' – they want high levels of service provision and customer care, but are inevitably frustrated when these are not delivered in practice. Sometimes this failure to deliver is due to poor performance, but it is also related to the unrealistic expectations that this group places on the council. The demands of this group often outstrip the capacity of the public sector to meet them. When decision making enters the trust judgement for the 'I have nots', it is as a concern that they should get their fair share of public spending and support.

Key services for this group are:

- housing issues
- benefit provision
- community services and facilities
- children's play areas
- street lighting

Improving customer contact and services, particularly with regard to housing and benefits, will be critical to building trust with this group. But perhaps just as importantly, councils may need to adopt a different customer service approach for the 'I have nots' based on empathy, explanation and problem solving. Contact staff faced with needs they cannot meet will need to be able to empathise with the problem, explain why the council cannot address it and help the 'I have nots' find alternative sources of help and support.

7 Implications and recommendations

The precise implementation of trust-building strategies will depend on the social context of a particular local authority area. Councils will need to tailor trust-building strategies according to their particular areas of weakness and the types of people they wish to appeal to, all the while having regard to particular local and community dynamics. But despite the immense diversity among even our small sample of local authorities, three overarching issues emerged from the research, which we believe have implications for building institutional kinds of trust in many other councils:

· first, that councils need to move from one-off problem-solving interactions with their citizens to ongoing, two-way relationships that allow for trust building
· second, that councils need to pay greater attention to the fairness of their decision-making processes and the way that their decisions are communicated, examining the role of issues such as scrutiny and transparency as well as executive decision-making powers
· third, that councillors should play a key role in closing the gap between the decision-making and personal spheres of trust

Addressing each of these challenges is likely to involve action at both the institutional and personal levels, taking both 'top-down' and 'bottom-up' approaches to building trust. If councils are successful in building trust, we can expect them to realise some of the benefits, such as greater willingness to forgive occasional mistakes, that we have outlined above. In addition, it may be possible that building trust in the council will have a spill-over effect into more generalised forms of trust among communities, leading to a greater sense of collective efficacy and reducing problems like violence and anti-social behaviour.

We explore some possible approaches to building trust below.

Relationship building

Most people contact their council only very occasionally when things go wrong, engaging in one-off problem-solving interactions. This kind of relationship does not create much space for trust formation and is likely to produce negative emotional experiences that undermine trust.

If local government wants to build trust, the first step is to develop a better kind of relationship with the people it serves. Our research suggests that these improved relationships will have to be long-term, consistent and characterised by honesty and reciprocity. They may also depend on local authorities promoting the image of their staff as being intrinsically motivated to help the public – portrayals of frontline public servants as little more than selfish 'producers' are unlikely to win trust for anyone.

Institutional factors do matter here, but they may not be critical. For instance, a strong and unified brand, combined with an attractive statement of values, seems likely to build some of the foundations for trust in frontline staff. Given the fact that the public sees local government as responsible for the actions of its service delivery partners, it seems particularly important to establish consistent sets of values and behaviours across partnerships, and ideally to have a single point of contact for all council services regardless of who delivers them. But institutional changes will build trust only if they are lived out in the everyday interactions between frontline staff and citizens.

At the interpersonal level of trust, an obvious approach to improving relationships with citizens would be to 'personalise' customer contact with local government. By giving every member of the public a named caseworker, councils could create the basis for a trusting personal relationship between members of the public and customer contact staff.

Neighbourhood police teams offer one example of this approach in action – providing local residents with the names and contact details of the officers responsible for their area and encouraging residents to contact their local teams with questions.

Training contact staff to be more emotionally intelligent, demonstrating concern and empathy for people's needs and problems, might go a long way towards building the emotional basis of trust. A trusting relationship will probably also have to involve trust from both parties – with the public accepting occasional lapses and mistakes, and the council being prepared to deal flexibly with the occasional missed payment or late form.

To maximise the chances of building trusting relationships, customer service teams probably need to adopt elements of the following approaches to interacting with the public:

· An approach to customer contact that appeals to the emotional basis of trust based on empathy, friendliness and explanation – staff need to display an acceptance of people's problems and offer an explanation of what the council can do and why its ability to help might be limited.
· A problem-solving approach in which someone's caseworker is able to link them to sources of help from across the council area – for instance helping someone who called the council find help from the police, the NHS trust or organisations from the voluntary sector. This might imply a single non-emergency contact centre for a whole locality.
· A proactive approach to service recovery – emphasising to a member of the public that their poor experience is not typical and offering them some form of redress as an indication that their experience was unusual.
· A degree of discretion over enforcing penalties – for instance for late payment of bills or rent. If a member of the public has a good record of payment but has missed a single instalment, customer contact staff should be able to delay penalties to show reciprocal trust.

All of this would need to be underpinned by a strong and well-understood set of public service values that were lived out in each interaction with contact staff and frontline deliverers working in every council service, no matter how that service is provided. This might be even more powerful if those values were agreed across whole sets of local service providers.

It will also be necessary to provide customised customer service approaches to different types of truster. For instance, the 'I have' group will generally want quick and easy transactional services over the phone or internet. Ambitious councils might want to try and use the web to engage them in decision making, encouraging 'we have' behaviour online. The 'I have nots' will often have multiple service needs best met through personal, joined-up interactions. The two 'we' groups may need information about upcoming decisions delivered online, in person and through the post, and information about how they can easily get involved.

This approach to customer service will require an initial investment to help staff develop new skills and expertise. But there are good reasons to assume that our approach may also deliver savings in the medium term by dealing with customer calls more effectively on the first contact. In any case, it seems unlikely to us that a case management approach would produce more calls – particularly if 'I haves' can increasingly be persuaded to use the internet. A case management approach should simply deal with the existing workload more effectively.

Elements of this approach are already in place in councils like the London Borough of Hammersmith and Fulham, which has used customer service data to redesign its customer contact services around the needs of different groups.[49]

Improving fairness

The perceived fairness of strategic spending and service decisions is a major issue for local government as a whole, despite many recent reforms that have sought to increase the openness and transparency of council governance. The immediate problem seems to be that the public has so little awareness of their council's decision-making processes that new approaches designed to increase openness and transparency simply do not register with local people.

This perception problem can be compounded by genuine examples of bad faith on the part of some councils. For instance, some authorities in our sample admitted to making the mistake of consulting over decisions which had, in reality, already been taken. This could lead to justifiable cynicism on the part of local people.

The ultimate goal for the councils in our sample was summed up by Solihull's former chief executive, Katherine Kerswell, who argues that her ultimate aim is to create a relationship in which the public 'may disagree with a decision, but they'll have listened and think "that's the best they can do for us"'.[50] Councils should respond to this challenge by placing a greater emphasis on the way they communicate their decisions, striving to communicate the procedural fairness of their institutions. They need to recognise that 'fairness' is not always the same as 'justice' – simply following the rules will not build trust unless those rules are widely accepted as being fair.

A first step towards improving trust in this area might be to create a local 'decision-making charter' to set out how the council will ensure that its decisions are taken in a fair and open way. This would work in much the same way as the lists of 'customer service promises' that many councils already use, emphasising the values that underpin a council's approach to governance and putting in place some of the institutional conditions for trust formation.

The charter could be included in council communications with the electorate and handed out to people who attend consultation meetings. Once a decision is taken, the council could show how the process conformed to the charter. Ideally, such a charter would be based on public consultation and have cross-party political support. It would need to emphasise some of the values of procedural fairness set out in chapter 1.

The list of potential attributes below recognises that the process of decision making is about much more than discussions in cabinet meetings – to seem fair, decisions need to involve scrutiny, broad debate and opportunities for redress:

· Decision makers will treat all local people equally in their deliberations.
· They will use the most accurate and up-to-date information to come to a decision.
· They will ensure that all voices are heard on the issue at hand, and seriously consider competing views.
· They will involve citizens directly in as many decisions as possible.
· They will subject decisions to appropriate scrutiny.
· There will be opportunities to review and appeal against the decision.

This charter should also set out how these decision-making processes are reflected in the structures of the council – highlighting procedures for consultation, scrutiny and appeal. Councils might also allow scrutiny committees to produce reports once decisions are taken that set out whether that decision complied with the council's decision-making charter. In addition, councils could use a decision-making charter to guarantee local people the right to participate in decision making, for instance through participatory budgeting.

It may also be possible to take a similar approach to decisions made about individuals by particular services. For instance, someone who is unable to get the windows in their council house repaired should at the very least be entitled to an explanation of why this is the case and why the council regards its decision as fair.

Councillors and trust

Politicians are in a unique position to build trust in the council. As elected representatives, they have the potential to create strong relationships with their constituents and to link the people in their ward to the council's strategic decision-making processes. In short, they should be able to act as the missing link between trust in people and trust in decision making.

There are currently a number of barriers to councillors assuming this kind of role. In policy terms, the role of backbench politicians has until very recently been underdeveloped – they have had only limited formal opportunities through full council and via scrutiny committees to represent the views of their constituents. In practical terms, many councillors are invisible in their local area, which means that they simply are not building long-term reciprocal relationships with many of their constituents.

In political terms, some councillors have fallen into the trap of promoting distrust in the local authority to win election. This means that when they do win power, they often inherit a damaged institution. There is a danger that some local political cultures might actively promote a downward spiral in trust in the very institution that parties seek to control.

The first of these problems – the lack of a clear role for backbenchers – is being tackled to some degree by proposals in the Local Government white paper and the Local Government and Public Involvement in Health bill.[51] Increasing power for scrutiny committees, community calls for action and the development of neighbourhood budgets all help to provide more opportunities for backbench activism. They also begin to bridge the gap between the personal trust people place in a good ward councillor and the trust they place in the council as a decision-making body. It may ultimately be the case that ward councillors need to be even more clearly identified as community champions, clearly demarcated from the decision-making executive.

This approach has been developed in some councils that have adopted directly elected mayors, with areas like Newham drawing a very clear distinction between the mayor's strategic decision-making powers and the role of councillors as either advocates or 'mini mayors' for their neighbourhoods.

These measures may go some way towards raising the profile of ward councillors but, ultimately, solving the second problem of visibility will require local politicians themselves to change the way they operate in their ward. Options for making councillors more visible include:

· Neighbourhood offices: Councillors could be supported by small constituency offices with perhaps one or two politically appointed members of staff who would coordinate ward-based consultations and political activity, help manage discretionary budgets and act as a 'one-stop shop' for local complaints and problems. This would help create a team of politicians and support staff who are clearly 'of the community' rather than the council.

· 'Patch walks': Councillors could become more proactive in walking their ward, perhaps with local service providers such as police officers or middle managers from the council's street scene team and housing managers. This would provide opportunities for them to meet constituents and answer questions.

These mechanisms seem likely to raise the profile of ward councillors while appealing to the public view that local politicians should be in touch with the issues the public thinks are important, and work in the interests of their neighbourhoods.

Finally, we have to overcome a political style that we have termed 'the problem paradigm', in which councillors primarily seek to identify constituent complaints and use them to run down trust in the council in order to win election. This attitude might be summed up as 'I want the council to be trusted when I'm in charge, but not when the opposition wins the election'. It is unsustainable partly because of the downward spiral of trust that it can encourage and partly because citizens are increasingly more likely to contact council call centres directly about their problems. This culture also holds councillors back from developing longer-term, more positive relationships with their constituents.

The idea of a local decision-making charter with cross-party support should encourage a more positive approach to politics by creating a core set of behaviours that all councillors can agree on. But ultimately we may need to go further and encourage a broader culture change in some council areas away from the minutiae of complaints towards the kind of long-term, two-way relationships that build trust.

This shift might be described as moving 'from problem-solving to place shaping'.[52] It implies that councillors increasingly need to talk as much about the future of their area and the ways in which they intend to improve it as they do about their role in dealing with short-term service delivery problems. Party political competition needs to be more about different values and visions, and less about scoring points against the other side.

Ultimately, fostering a shift to a more positive and visible role for councillors might be the single most important thing local government can do to build trust.

For much of the past decade, public service reform has focused on doing things and not the way they are done. This approach has delivered significant improvements in local government services, but there is little evidence that it has increased our trust in governing institutions.

This report points in a fresh direction, showing how councils need to take a more subtle and balanced approach to governance and service delivery if they want to move beyond improvement towards building a new kind of relationship with their citizens. Our message is simple – relationships with citizens are built through process and interaction, so creating fair and engaging processes matters just as much as delivering high-quality services.

The reward for getting those processes right is a kind of broad institutional trust that we believe will lead to more useful and fulfilling interactions between the public and local authorities. This is not the trust that a child puts in a parent – it would be undesirable and unrealistic to return to a supposedly golden age of deference. Rather, we need to create a more mature trust relationship between citizen and state, with each treating the other as a mature, intelligent and competent partner in improving quality of life in communities.

This kind of relationship is critical to the next stage of local government's development: a stage that will be characterised by devolution, citizen empowerment and attempts to lead and shape whole local areas.

Personalising services offers part of the answer to building greater trust by helping professionals develop deeper and more conversational relationships with the people they serve. But we need to acknowledge the limits of this approach. Personalisation might just exacerbate the problem of the public trusting professionals, but not the institutions they work for.

Many local government services cannot realistically be personalised – from regeneration to refuse collection, they are inherently collective. Councillors need to become the face of these collective decision-making processes, linking people into robust, fair and widely understood processes of decision making about the local area.

National politicians, regulators and opinion formers can also help to develop a mature trust relationship by recognising the strong body of evidence that suggests that there is a public service ethos that drives staff to help the public. Recent survey work from the University of Manchester concludes that there is 'something special' about the high levels of altruism demonstrated by the current generation of young people entering public service.[53]

Our research suggests that, for whatever reason, the public believes that public service workers are motivated by a large degree of goodwill. Perhaps this is simply a way of justifying their dependency on public services; perhaps it is the result of genuinely positive experience. In either case, it would do no harm if we acknowledged and promoted the fact that the public appears to be right.

Appendix 1: Methodology

In addition to a literature review, this project used three primary research methodologies to map trust in each of the four local authority areas:

- focus groups with members of the public to understand the trust relationship they wanted to build with the council
- workshops with council staff to understand how they saw trust issues in their area
- depth interviews with senior council officers and politicians

This combination of research methodologies was expected to yield an in-depth understanding of trust from both inside and outside the council.

Focus groups

Demos and the qualitative research company Spiral conducted 20 focus groups across the four councils with the aim of developing a citizen segmentation around trust, based on attitudes, behaviour and socio-demographics. The output has been a set of nationally useful 'truster' typologies, and analysis of specific trust issues in participating areas.

Although we aimed to secure a sample that was broadly representative of the UK's population, we were less interested in socio-demographic factors than in understanding broad attitudes to trust across society. We took this decision based on quantitative Ipsos MORI work, which showed that:

attitudes to trust do not relate strongly to standard socio-demographic factors, but are more likely to be based on a range of general values and beliefs about the public sector.[54]

Our goal, then, was to try and establish what those value and beliefs might be. The focus groups therefore aimed to answer four research questions:

1 How do people form trust relationships in their broadest sense, eg with business, their neighbours, strangers?
2 What factors drive people to trust more or less in those relationships?
3 How do they specifically form trust relationships with their council? To what extent is this based on services or wider factors such as politics, fairness or public purpose? What services are most important in forming trust? Do people trust the institution or people within it? What impact do partnerships have?
4 What kind of trust relationship would people like with their council? What factors drive them to trust more or less in the council? For instance, what is the importance of information, knowing what the council does, voting in local elections, knowing your councillor?

Sample

The overall sample was recruited to be approximately representative of the UK population aged over 25. Recruitment was balanced to reflect local demographics and ensure a good coverage of different wards. Quotas were used to recruit a spread of ages, lifestages, socio-economic groups and private accommodation versus council dwellings. Profiling quotas were also used to identify people's attitudes to trust in the local authority, establishing whether they were generally likely to trust or not, and whether their levels of civic engagement were high or low.

In addition to standard group discussions, we used three other focus group techniques during the fieldwork. First, network research groups worked by recruiting a 'seed' representing a particular truster type (eg high trust and high civic engagement), and building a group using the seed's social network. These were essentially groups of friends and neighbours aimed at providing insights into the way that social groups influence trust relationships with the council.

Second, we also carried out one conflict group, in which we recruited two different truster types and used their conflicting views to help clarify differences of opinion. After piloting our methodology in Lewisham, we decided to discontinue the conflict group methodology. Participants proved reluctant to express conflicting views in public, meaning that the process provided few new insights. The conflict group was replaced by a third technique – interviews with pairs of friends to allow for in-depth examination of particular truster types.

A full list of the groups carried out follows below:

Lewisham (September 2006)

· two 90-minute group discussions
· one 90-minute conflict group discussion
· one network research session

Wakefield (November 2006)

· two 90-minute group discussions
· three 75-minute friendship pairs
· one network research session

Solihull (December 2006)

· two 90-minute group discussions
· three 75-minute friendship pairs
· one network research session

Sunderland (January 2007)

· two 90-minute group discussions
· two network research sessions

Staff workshops

Demos ran eight workshops with council staff across the four local authority areas to understand their views on trust – did they feel trusted and did they feel trust was useful? We also hoped that dealing with articulate groups of public servants would provide more general insights into trust and its formation.

In each area we conducted one workshop with frontline staff – defined as people who deliver services directly to the public – and one with middle managers. Groups were selected by participating councils in consultation with Demos researchers and conducted on council premises.

These sessions were based around workbooks, which participants were asked to complete in pairs. The process was facilitated throughout by two researchers, who sat with groups to capture their responses to the workbooks.

The research questions for this session, reflected in the workbooks, were:

1 How do council staff define trust?
2 What kind of people do they trust and what characteristics do those people have?
3 What institutions do they trust and why (a list of 20 public, private and voluntary sector organisations was provided as stimulus)?
4 Do they think the public trusts: participants personally, their department or service, or the council as a whole?
5 When has trust made a concrete difference in their daily lives and what benefits has it provided?

Depth interviews

Using the same research questions, we interviewed ten councillors and 17 senior officers across our local authorities, including the chief executives of all four councils. Given that councillors have a critical role to play in developing trust with the public, we intend to investigate their views and attitudes further in the next stage of the research process.

Notes

1   Hutton, foreword in O'Hara, *Trust: From Socrates to spin*.

2   See for instance Fukuyama, *Trust*.

3   Compact Oxford English Dictionary (online edition), see
     www.askoxford.com/concise_oed/trust?view=uk (accessed
     27 May 2008).

4   Only 24 per cent of people in the UK trust the government, one
     of the lowest figures in Europe. In a league table of the EU25,
     the UK comes joint 22nd with France. Only Hungary and
     Poland score lower. See *Eurobarometer 66*.

5   Bromley, Curtice and Seyd, *Is Britain Facing a Crisis of Democracy?*

6   Ipsos MORI surveys cited in Lyons, *Place Shaping*.

7   MORI poll, Nov 2006, cited at
     www.bma.org.uk/ap.nsf/Content/DoctorsPublicPU (accessed 26
     May 2008).

8   Ipsos MORI, *Survey of Attitudes Towards Conduct in Public Life
     2006*. The survey sets out trust data for Great Britain in 2004 and
     2006.

9   For a consideration of this argument, see Harkin and Skidmore,
     Grown Up Trust.

10   For a summary of these arguments, see Taylor-Gooby, 'The
     efficiency/trust dilemma'.

11 Between 2002 and 2004, the number of councils rated 'good' or 'excellent' in the Comprehensive Performance Assessment (CPA) increased from 76 to 101, while overall satisfaction levels fell from 65 per cent to 53 per cent between 2000 and 2006.

12 Lyons, *Place Shaping*.

13 Machiavelli, *The Prince*.

14 Misztal, *Trust in Modern Societies*.

15 The literature is summarised in Perri 6 et al, *Managing Networks of Twenty First Century Organisations*.

16 See, for instance, O'Hara, *Trust*.

17 The literature is ably summarised in Pearce, 'Rethinking fairness'.

18 Leventhal, summarised in Tyler et al, *Social Justice in a Diverse Society*.

19 Standards Board for England and Ipsos MORI, *Public Perceptions of Ethics*.

20 Rahn and Rudolph, 'A tale of political trust in American cities'.

21 Hong and Bohnet, *Status and Distrust*.

22 MORI, *Trust in Public Institutions*.

23 Ibid.

24 See, for instance, Ibid.; and Ipsos MORI, *Survey of Attitudes Towards Conduct in Public Life 2006*.

25 Rahn and Rudolph, 'A tale of political trust in American cities'.

26 See, for instance, Johnson and Grayson, 'Cognitive and affective trust in service relationships'.

27 Schwartz, 'Emotion, cognition and decision making'.

28 Bohnet and Huck, *Repetition and Reputation*.

29 See, for instance, Pearce, 'Rethinking fairness'.

30 Axelrod, *The Evolution of Cooperation*.

31 Sampson, 'Networks and neighbourhoods'.

32 Interview with B Quirk, Jul 2006.

33 For more information see http://campaigns.lga.gov.uk/
    reputation/home/ (accessed 20 Dec 2007).

34 Argument adapted from Wan de Walle and Bouckaert, 'Public
    service performance and trust in government'; and Firth,
    Professorial Fellowship.

35 See the Audit Commission website, www.audit-
    commission.gov.uk/cpa/ (accessed 27 May 2008).

36 Taylor-Gooby, 'The efficiency/trust dilemma'.

37 See for example Seligman, *The Problem of Trust*.

38 See for instance Newton and Norris, 'Confidence in public
    institutions'.

39 Ipsos MORI, *State of the Nation Report*.

40 Ipsos MORI, *Survey of Attitudes Towards Conduct in Public Life
    2006*.

41 Taylor and Williams, *Perceptions of Local Government in England*.

42 Borins, *The Challenge of Innovating in Government*.

43 Ipsos MORI, 'Many councillors "divorced" from the electorate',
    a survey of 1067 adults aged 15 plus across Great Britain.

44 This finding is echoed by Taylor and Williams in *Perceptions of Local Government in England*.

45 Ibid.

46 Ibid.

47 Lyons, *Place Shaping*.

48 MORI, *Trust in Public Institutions*.

49 For more information on Hammersmith and Fulham's experience, see Naylor, 'Customer-driven service design'.

50 Interview with K Kerswell, Nov 2006.

51 See www.communities.gov.uk/publications/ localgovernment/strongprosperous and www.publications.parliament.uk/ pa/cm200607/cmbills/ 016/2007016.pdf (both accessed 27 May 2008).

52 We are indebted to Paul Cotterill for this handy formulation.

53 John and Johnson, 'Is there still a public service ethos?'.

54 Ipsos MORI, *Trust in Public Institutions: New findings*.

References

Axelrod, R, *The Evolution of Cooperation* (New York: Basic Books, 1984).

Bohnet, I and Huck, S, *Repetition and Reputation: Implications for trust and trustworthiness in the short and in the long run*, working paper no RWP03-048 (Cambridge, MA: Kennedy School of Government, Harvard University, 2003), available at http://ksgnotes1.harvard.edu/Research/wpaper.nsf/pubwzAuthor?OpenForm&Start=1&Count=1700&Expand=12&Seq=1 (accessed 26 May 2008).

Borins, S, *The Challenge of Innovating in Government*, 2nd edn (Toronto: IBM Centre for the Business of Government, University of Toronto, 2006).

Bromley, C, Curtice, J and Seyd, B, *Is Britain Facing a Crisis of Democracy?* working paper, Centre for Research into Elections and Social Trends (Crest), available at www.crest.ox.ac.uk (accessed 26 May 2008).

Eurobarometer 66: Public opinion in the European Union. United Kingdom National Report (Brussels: European Commission, Autumn 2006), available at http://ec.europa.eu/public_opinion/archives/eb/eb66/eb66_uk_nat.pdf (accessed 26 May 2008).

Firth, D, *Professorial Fellowship: Models, measurement and inference in social research; full research report*, ESRC End of Award Report, RES-153-25-0036 (Swindon: Economic and Social Research Council, 2007).

Fukuyama, F, *Trust: The social virtues and the creation of prosperity* (London: Hamish Hamilton, 1995).

Harkin, J and Skidmore, P, *Grown Up Trust* (London: Demos, 2003).

Hong, K and Bohnet, I, *Status and Distrust: The relevance of inequality and betrayal aversion*, working paper no RWP04-041 (Cambridge, MA: Kennedy School of Government, Harvard University, 2004), available at http://ksgnotes1.harvard.edu/Research/wpaper.nsf/pubwzAuthor?OpenForm&Start=1&Count=1700&Expand=12&Seq=1 (accessed 26 May 2008).

Ipsos MORI, 'Many councillors "divorced" from the electorate', May 2002, available at www.ipsos-mori.com/content/many-councillors-divorced-from-the-electorate.ashx (accessed 27 May 2008).

Ipsos MORI, *State of the Nation Report*, 2004, available at www.ipsos-mori.com/content/state-of-the-nation-report.ashx (accessed 27 May 2008).

Ipsos MORI, *Survey of Attitudes Towards Conduct in Public Life 2006* (London: Committee for Standards in Public Life, 2006).

Ipsos MORI, *Trust in Public Institutions: New findings, national quantitative survey*, n.d. available at www.ipsos-mori.com/_assets/publications/pdf/omnibus3.pdf (accessed 27 May 2008).

John, P and Johnson, M, 'Is there still a public service ethos?' in Park, A et al (eds), *British Social Attitudes: The 24th report* (London: Sage, 2008).

Johnson, D and Grayson, K, 'Cognitive and affective trust in service relationships', *Journal of Business Research* 58 (2005).

Lyons, M, *Place Shaping: A shared ambition for the future of local government*, final report (London: TSO, 2007), available at: www.webarchive.org.uk/pan/15454/20070428/www.lyonsinquiry. org.uk/docs/final-complete.pdf (accessed 26 May 2008).

Machiavelli, N, *The Prince*, written c. 1505, published 1515, transl. WK Marriott, 1908, available at www.constitution.org/mac/ prince00.htm (accessed 26 May 2008).

Misztal, B, *Trust in Modern Societies* (Cambridge: Polity Press, 1996).

MORI, *Trust in Public Institutions*, n.d., see www.ipsos-mori.com/ _assets/publications/pdf/final.pdf (accessed 27 May 2008).

Naylor, C, 'Customer-driven service design' in Parker, S and Parker, S (eds), *Unlocking Innovation: Why citizens hold the key to public service reform* (London: Demos, 2007).

Newton, K and Norris, P, 'Confidence in public institutions: faith, culture or performance' in Pharr, S and Puttnam, R (eds), *Disaffected Democracies* (Princeton: Princeton University Press, 2000).

O'Hara, K, *Trust: From Socrates to spin* (Colchester: Icon, 2004).

Pearce, N, 'Rethinking fairness', *Public Policy Review* 14, no 1 (Mar–May 2007), available at www.blackwell-synergy.com/doi/ abs/10.1111/j.1744-540X.2007.00458.x (accessed 22 Jan 2008).

Perri 6 et al, *Managing Networks of Twenty First Century Organisations* (Basingstoke: Palgrave Macmillan, 2006).

Rahn, W and Rudolph, T, 'A tale of political trust in American cities', *Public Opinion Quarterly* 69, no 4 (Winter 2005).

Sampson, R, 'Networks and neighbourhoods' in McCarthy, H, Miller, P and Skidmore, P (eds), *Network Logic: Who governs in an interconnected world?* (London: Demos, 2003).

Schwartz, N, 'Emotion, cognition and decision making', *Cognition and Emotion* 14, no 4 (2000).

Seligman, A, *The Problem of Trust* (Princeton: Princeton University Press, 1997).

Standards Board for England and Ipsos MORI, *Public Perceptions of Ethics* (London: Standards Board, 2006).

Taylor, S and Williams, B, *Perceptions of Local Government in England: Key findings from qualitative research* (London: BMG Research Ltd, for Department for Communities and Local Government, Oct 2006), available at www.communities.gov.uk/ publications/localgovernment/perceptionslocal (accessed 26 May 2008).

Taylor-Gooby, P, 'The efficiency/trust dilemma', *Health, Risk and Society* 8, no 2 (2006).

Tyler, TR et al, *Social Justice in a Diverse Society* (Oxford: Westview Press, 1997).

Wan de Walle, S and Bouckaert, G, 'Public service performance and trust in government: the problem of causality', *International Journal of Public Administration* 26, no 8&9 (2003).

Demos – Licence to Publish

The work (as defined below) is provided under the terms of this licence ('licence'). The work is protected by copyright and/or other applicable law. Any use of the work other than as authorized under this licence is prohibited. By exercising any rights to the work provided here, you accept and agree to be bound by the terms of this licence. Demos grants you the rights contained here in consideration of your acceptance of such terms and conditions.

1   Definitions

A   **'Collective Work'** means a work, such as a periodical issue, anthology or encyclopedia, in which the Work in its entirety in unmodified form, along with a number of other contributions, constituting separate and independent works in themselves, are assembled into a collective whole. A work that constitutes a Collective Work will not be considered a Derivative Work (as defined below) for the purposes of this Licence.

B   **'Derivative Work'** means a work based upon the Work or upon the Work and other pre-existing works, such as a musical arrangement, dramatization, fictionalization, motion picture version, sound recording, art reproduction, abridgment, condensation, or any other form in which the Work may be recast, transformed, or adapted, except that a work that constitutes a Collective Work or a translation from English into another language will not be considered a Derivative Work for the purpose of this Licence.

C   **'Licensor'** means the individual or entity that offers the Work under the terms of this Licence.

D   **'Original Author'** means the individual or entity who created the Work.

E   **'Work'** means the copyrightable work of authorship offered under the terms of this Licence.

F   **'You'** means an individual or entity exercising rights under this Licence who has not previously violated the terms of this Licence with respect to the Work,or who has received express permission from Demos to exercise rights under this Licence despite a previous violation.

2   Fair Use Rights

Nothing in this licence is intended to reduce, limit, or restrict any rights arising from fair use, first sale or other limitations on the exclusive rights of the copyright owner under copyright law or other applicable laws.

3   Licence Grant

Subject to the terms and conditions of this Licence, Licensor hereby grants You a worldwide, royalty-free, non-exclusive,perpetual (for the duration of the applicable copyright) licence to exercise the rights in the Work as stated below:

A   to reproduce the Work, to incorporate the Work into one or more Collective Works, and to reproduce the Work as incorporated in the Collective Works;

B   to distribute copies or phonorecords of, display publicly,perform publicly, and perform publicly by means of a digital audio transmission the Work including as incorporated in Collective Works; The above rights may be exercised in all media and formats whether now known or hereafter devised.The above rights include the right to make such modifications as are technically necessary to exercise the rights in other media and formats. All rights not expressly granted by Licensor are hereby reserved.

4   Restrictions

The licence granted in Section 3 above is expressly made subject to and limited by the following restrictions:

A   You may distribute,publicly display, publicly perform, or publicly digitally perform the Work only under the terms of this Licence, and You must include a copy of, or the Uniform Resource Identifier for, this Licence with every copy or phonorecord of the Work You distribute, publicly display,publicly perform, or publicly digitally perform.You may not offer or impose any terms on the Work that alter or restrict the terms of this Licence or the recipients' exercise of the rights granted hereunder.You may not sublicence the Work.You must keep intact all notices that refer to this Licence and to the disclaimer of warranties.You may not distribute, publicly display, publicly perform, or publicly digitally perform the Work with any technological measures that control access or use of the Work in a manner inconsistent with the terms of this Licence Agreement.The above applies to the Work as incorporated in a Collective Work, but this does not require the Collective Work apart from the Work itself to be made subject to the terms of this Licence. If You create a Collective Work, upon notice from any Licencor You must, to the extent practicable, remove from the Collective Work any reference to such Licensor or the Original Author, as requested.

B   You may not exercise any of the rights granted to You in Section 3 above in any manner that is primarily intended for or directed toward commercial advantage or private monetary compensation.The exchange of the Work for other copyrighted works by means of digital filesharing or otherwise shall not be considered to be intended for or directed toward commercial advantage or private monetary compensation, provided there is no payment of any monetary compensation in connection with the exchange of copyrighted works.

c   If you distribute, publicly display, publicly perform, or publicly digitally perform the Work or any Collective Works,You must keep intact all copyright notices for the Work and give the Original Author credit reasonable to the medium or means You are utilizing by conveying the name (or pseudonym if applicable) of the Original Author if supplied; the title of the Work if supplied. Such credit may be implemented in any reasonable manner; provided, however, that in the case of a Collective Work, at a minimum such credit will appear where any other comparable authorship credit appears and in a manner at least as prominent as such other comparable authorship credit.

5   Representations, Warranties and Disclaimer

A   By offering the Work for public release under this Licence, Licensor represents and warrants that, to the best of Licensor's knowledge after reasonable inquiry:

i   Licensor has secured all rights in the Work necessary to grant the licence rights hereunder and to permit the lawful exercise of the rights granted hereunder without You having any obligation to pay any royalties, compulsory licence fees, residuals or any other payments;

ii The Work does not infringe the copyright, trademark, publicity rights, common law rights or any other right of any third party or constitute defamation, invasion of privacy or other tortious injury to any third party.

B   except as expressly stated in this licence or otherwise agreed in writing or required by applicable law,the work is licenced on an 'as is'basis,without warranties of any kind, either express or implied including,without limitation,any warranties regarding the contents or accuracy of the work.

6   Limitation on Liability

Except to the extent required by applicable law, and except for damages arising from liability to a third party resulting from breach of the warranties in section 5, in no event will licensor be liable to you on any legal theory for any special, incidental,consequential, punitive or exemplary damages arising out of this licence or the use of the work, even if licensor has been advised of the possibility of such damages.

7   Termination

A   This Licence and the rights granted hereunder will terminate automatically upon any breach by You of the terms of this Licence. Individuals or entities who have received Collective Works from You under this Licence,however, will not have their licences terminated provided such individuals or entities remain in full compliance with those licences. Sections 1, 2, 5, 6, 7, and 8 will survive any termination of this Licence.

B   Subject to the above terms and conditions, the licence granted here is perpetual (for the duration of the applicable copyright in the Work). Notwithstanding the above, Licensor reserves the right to release the Work under different licence terms or to stop distributing the Work at any time; provided, however that any such election will not serve to withdraw this Licence (or any other licence that has been, or is required to be, granted under the terms of this Licence), and this Licence will continue in full force and effect unless terminated as stated above.

8   Miscellaneous

A   Each time You distribute or publicly digitally perform the Work or a Collective Work, Demos offers to the recipient a licence to the Work on the same terms and conditions as the licence granted to You under this Licence.

B   If any provision of this Licence is invalid or unenforceable under applicable law, it shall not affect the validity or enforceability of the remainder of the terms of this Licence, and without further action by the parties to this agreement, such provision shall be reformed to the minimum extent necessary to make such provision valid and enforceable.

C   No term or provision of this Licence shall be deemed waived and no breach consented to unless such waiver or consent shall be in writing and signed by the party to be charged with such waiver or consent.

D   This Licence constitutes the entire agreement between the parties with respect to the Work licensed here.There are no understandings, agreements or representations with respect to the Work not specified here. Licensor shall not be bound by any additional provisions that may appear in any communication from You.This Licence may not be modified without the mutual written agreement of Demos and You.